Walking Guen, Again

Gary Williams

SUSPENSE PUBLISHING

WALKING GUEN, AGAIN
By Gary Williams

PAPERBACK EDITION
* * * * *
PUBLISHED BY:
Suspense Publishing

COPYRIGHT
2019 by Gary S. Williams and Vicky W. Knerly Partnership

PUBLISHING HISTORY:
Suspense Publishing, Digital Copy, April 2019

Cover Design: Shannon Raab
Cover & Interior Photographer: Gary Williams
Paws: Serhii Brovko / iStock

ISBN: ISBN: 978-0-578-43070-6

Walking Guen, Again

Gary Williams

Praising Guen

"Gary and Guen's conversations are a delight. I found myself chuckling throughout the book. I hope this book is the first of many."

"A dog lover's must! Can't wait for the next one!"

"This is such a charming and entertaining book! This is the perfect combination—an excellent author and a super cute and spoiled pupper!"

"Delightful read! Looking forward to Walking Guen Part II!"

"Eight paws up! Such fun and laughter; witty banter that most of us have with our fur babies but don't write down."

"I enjoyed every minute of this book and the sweet pictures of Guen just put the icing on the cake!"

"Very funny and entertaining! Gary and Guen are two of my favorites and I enjoyed reading their book. Humor runs through their veins. I like to laugh, and they do make me laugh!"

"Walking Guen is a great find for the person who loves dogs, humor, and history."

"This book is so much fun to read. I'm not sure who's funnier....Gary or Guen."

"The funny, witty and even hilarious conversations will make you smile and at times you will find yourself laughing out loud. This is a fun book that anyone would enjoy."

"Witty conversations between a dog and her best friend! Guen and Gary take daily walks through St Augustine and have the most entertaining and educational chats. This is a lovely collection of some of those chats, and I'm looking forward to the next installment. If you like dogs, you'll love this book."

"This book lifts your spirits."

" 'Walking Guen' is a delightful, uplifting read. Really love the witty 'Guen' and her human Gary on their interesting walks around St Augustine bantering back and forth from historical facts to unusual finds along the way."

A Little History

For those new to this series, I'm Gary, and my yellow Labrador retriever is Guen, pronounced Gwen. Guen is short for Guinevere, which I misspelled with an "e" upon the first visit to the vet. Sure, I could have corrected it, but I let it slide. Guen, with the unique spelling, seemed to suit her.

More than five years ago, we moved to St. Augustine, a quaint historic town in northeast Florida. As I took Guen on walks through the streets, we had frivolous conversations. Yes, dogs talk if you listen hard enough. Our one rule was to avoid hot issues: no religion, politics, or other emotionally charged topics. I posted these walks and conversations on numerous St. Augustine-centric social media sites and, to my amazement, Guen developed a following, mainly for her snarky attitude, and the way she sometimes one-ups me. Okay, it happens more than sometimes. In fact, she usually gets the best of me, but I digress. Anyway, in late 2018, we published the first "Walking Guen" book, and the rest is history. Seriously, it's in the past so, yeah, it's history.

Anyway, we welcome you to come along on more walks in this second book. Hopefully, our conversations will make you smile and distract you from everyday life for a while. God knows, we all need the occasional distraction to keep us sane. Then again, this sage advice is coming from a man who talks to his dog.

~Gary & Guen

June 8, 2017

While walking Guen through the soggy, historic streets of St. Augustine this morning, we came to a fork in the road. We didn't take it. The End.

Actually, there's more.

"So where do you think this came from?" Guen asked.

"Most likely, someone accidentally threw it out in the trash and it fell out of the can."

"I don't think so. I bet a mega-billionaire was flying over St. Augustine, about to eat a gourmet meal, when he asked for a spork. Instead, he was handed a fork. He was so mad that he threw the fork out of the window, and it landed here on Riberia Street."

I nodded. "Yes, Guen, because mega-billionaires prefer sporks."

"It's a trendy thing. You really should keep up with pop culture."

June 14, 2017

While walking Guen through the historic streets of St. Augustine this morning, she found a cushion on Sevilla Street. She turned and said, "This reminds me, I once knew a guy who owned a drinking establishment and—"

"You knew a guy who owned a bar?"

"I have friends. Anyway, his patrons complained that his bar chairs were uncomfortable, so he added cushions. But then business dropped off because he kept referring to the cushions as stool softeners."

I looked at her in silence for a long moment. "Keep walking, Guen."

June 19, 2017

While walking Guen through the historic streets of St. Augustine this morning, she stopped to look at a large house for sale built in 1903. "And you're sure they won't take an offer of 12 dog treats?"

"Guen, they're asking $1.2 million."

"Yeah, but a dozen treats has a street value of, like, 50 *tra*billion dollars."

"Okay, Guen, I'll submit your offer. We'll see if they accept it."

She grinned. "They will. Then I'll be livin' large."

"News flash. You already are."

June 22, 2017

While walking Guen through the historic streets of St. Augustine this morning, we were on King Street when she asked, "What's this place?"

"Markland. It was the home of Dr. Andrew Anderson. In 1885, Henry Flagler met with Dr. Anderson and others here to plan the construction of the opulent Hotel Ponce de León, just east of Markland."

"I love the way they named homes back in the day."

I nodded. "You mean like Markland, Kirkside, Tara?"

"Yeah. I think we should consider naming our place. We could call it 'Guen Manor.' "

"I have a better one. Since we live at the back of the neighborhood, how 'bout the 'Mooch Pooch Caboose'?"

"Goin' out on a limb here, but I think 'Guen Manor' has a much more regal ring to it."

June 25, 2017

While walking Guen through the historic streets of St. Augustine this morning, she paused to rest on Carrera Street. "Why are you in such a good mood today?" she asked.

"Just finished the draft of our next novel."

"Did you take my suggestion and include a superhero Dachshund named Edgar who wears a purple fedora and has a magic wand for a tail that he uses to help pets in distress?"

"No, no we didn't, Guen."

"Then I don't know why you're so happy with yourself. The story can't be *that* good."

June 26, 2017

While walking Guen through the historic streets of St. Augustine this morning, we were on Carrera Street when I said, "See that two-story red house? In the mid-1890s, Henry Flagler's gardener lived there. The gardener's young son used to play with Ida Alice, Flagler's second wife, who was diagnosed as mentally ill. The boy would climb trees to retrieve Ida Alice's pet canary, which frequently escaped from its cage."

She looked at me with doubt. "In summation, you're telling me the son of Flagler's gardener use to scale trees for Henry's mentally ill wife to retrieve her Houdini-like bird?"

"Well, when you say it like that, it does sound odd."

"Geez, no wonder you write fiction." She shook her head.

"I swear it's all true!"

June 28, 2017

While walking Guen through the historic streets of St. Augustine this morning, we were at the east end of Saragossa Street when she started giggling.

"What?" I asked.

She pointed to the big yellow sign, then looked down and kept laughing.

I looked up. "I don't get what's so funny about—" I cut myself off and shook my head. "Just stop yourself, Guen."

June 29, 2017

While walking Guen through the historic streets of St. Augustine this morning, we were at the corner of Orange Street and Sevilla Street when Guen turned to me. "Why is my name spelled 'Guen' instead of the normal 'Gwen'?"

"For one, you're not normal. And two, you were named after Guinevere from Arthur and the Knights of the Round Table legend. But the first time I took you to the vet, I gave them the wrong spelling. I told them 'G-u-e-n' instead of 'G-u-i-n' and it's stuck ever since."

"Wait, so I was named after a queen?"

"Yep."

"Oh, I can live with that," she nodded.

June 30, 2017

While walking Guen through the historic streets of St. Augustine this morning, we arrived at the First United Methodist Church parking lot on the corner of King Street and Riberia Street.

"These post-rain ponds are fantastic!" Guen exclaimed. Her eyes widened. "Tomorrow we need to bring some pool toys for me to play with."

"I don't think so, Guen. Your teeth and claws don't mix well with thin vinyl."

She shook her head. "I was referring to our cats."

"Yeah, I can see it now. They'd be riding on your back like a dog ferry."

"Um, let's strike that idea," she relented.

July 3, 2017

While walking Guen through the historic streets of St. Augustine this morning, we were on Sevilla Street near the perimeter wall of Flagler College when Guen stopped. "I smell water."

"Of course you do. The swimming pool is not far over the wall."

"Henry Flagler built a swimming pool here?"

"No, it was a later addition. But Flagler did build a swimming pool inside the Hotel Alcazar, now Lightner Museum, across the street. As a matter of fact, at the time, it was the world's largest indoor swimming pool. They had daily water shows and daring daredevils who would dive from the grand balcony three floors above."

She glared at me in disbelief. "You've been taking me to tromp around in rain puddles when there are two swimming pools nearby?"

"Well, the indoor pool is gone. It's now a café."

"All the more reason to take me!"

July 5, 2017

W hile walking Guen through the historic streets of St. Augustine this morning, we were on Almeria Street when we spotted a toilet by the side of the road.

"Look. The sign says, 'Will work for free.' Not a bad deal. Hard to get good help these days," she said.

"I wonder if this is related to the mysterious theft of the toilets from the police station."

Guen nodded. "I heard the cops have nothing to go on."

19

July 7, 2017

While walking Guen through the historic, borderline-tropical streets of St. Augustine this morning, we were at the north end of Sevilla Street when Guen turned to me. "So when were you going to tell me about the 'Pancakes with Santa' Christmas-in-July event tomorrow morning at Fire Station 1 on Malaga Street?"

"It costs $8. You don't have $8."

"But you do. And it'll save you money."

I cocked my head. "Oh, it will?"

"Yes, because I won't chew up your $70 New Balance tennis shoes. Thus, you'll have a savings of $62."

I shook my head. "This must be that Common Core math I've heard so much about. Now I know why everyone hates it."

July 10, 2017

While walking Guen through the historic streets of St. Augustine this morning, we were in the courtyard of Fire Station 1 on Malaga Street when I threw up my hands in frustration. "Yeah, I know it's a fountain, and that it's tradition to toss in money to make a wish. What I don't understand is why you need $20?"

She turned toward the Fire Station bays. "Well, duh. I really, *really* want my wish to come true."

July 11. 2017

While walking Guen through the historic streets of St. Augustine this morning, we were between Francis Field and the Public Parking Garage when a loud boom caused us both to jump. Now, we've become accustomed to the mock cannon firing from the Castillo, but this explosion rocked the air and set off car alarms nearby.

"I think a transformer just blew, Guen."

She didn't respond.

"Guen? You okay?"

"Yeah, just checking to make sure all my fur is still attached."

I pointed, eyes wide. "Oh, my God! You've got a bald spot on your back!"

She whipped around. "Where? I don't see it?!"

By then, I was laughing.

She glared at me with narrowed eyes. "You're not funny."

July 12, 2017

Before taking Guen on a walk through the historic streets of St. Augustine this morning, I applied ample amounts of insect repellent. We were on Sevilla Street when Guen commented, "Are we playing Harry Potter this morning?"

"What are you talking about?"

She pointed to my now-oily skin. "You obviously belong to the House of Slatherin."

July 13, 2017

While walking Guen through the historic, toasty streets of St. Augustine this morning, we were on Almeria Street when she began to giggle.

"What's so funny?"

"I still remember the twisted expression on your face this morning when you took your first sip of coffee."

"That's because I didn't realize you'd replaced the sugar bowl with salt. Why would you do such a thing?"

"Because it's that day. You know, when you play practical jokes on people."

"You mean April Fool's Day? But it's July 13th!"

"Yes, but since one human year equals seven dog years, it's unfair that I only get to celebrate it once a year. So I've implemented the 7-day April Fool's Day year."

"You know, using that logic, each year you should have 7 birthdays, 7 Christmases, etc."

Her eyes lit up in anticipation.

"Dear God, what have I done?" I said, slapping my forehead.

July 14, 2017

While walking Guen through the historic, equatorial-like, heated streets of St. Augustine this morning, Guen said, "There's a lot of people walking their dogs this morning. Do you realize we've come across an Irish Setter, an English Bulldog, and a Scottish Terrier? It's like we've taken a trip to the United Kingdom."

"Pretty cool, huh?" I said.

"Right. Cheerio, mate!"

"Stop it."

Then, in a strange alignment of the universe, we met a nice woman named Kay who follows Guen on Facebook and has a decidedly British accent.

Afterward, Guen said, "Now, if I could only meet James Bond, my morning would be perfect."

"Um, Guen, you know he's just a fictional character."

"So *you* say."

July 15, 2017

While walking Guen through the historic, clammy streets of St. Augustine this morning, we were on Carrera Street when Guen said, "I proclaim this National Knick-Knack Paddywhack Day."

I looked at her with confusion. "Why?"

"Seriously?"

"What?" I exclaimed.

"You know, for a writer, you're not very sharp. Just say the second line."

"Ooooooh, now I get it."

"I doubt it," Guen said, shaking her head back and forth.

July 19, 2017

While walking Guen through the historic streets of St. Augustine this morning, we were on Cuna Street when she asked excitedly, "How many more days? How many more days?"

"In 31 days, the new Flagler College students arrive."

"Yippee! One month from today I get to tell them that I'm a Bolivian Lollygagger. I can't wait."

"Guen, you do appreciate the incoming freshmen as something more than targets for your amusement, right?"

"Of course, they bring life and vitality to our old city. Oh, and I thought up another breed to tell them: Saskatchewan Shawshank."

I shook my head. "Sounds like a Canadian movie sequel."

"Ah, but this time it's a comedy."

July 22, 2017

While walking Guen through the historic streets of St. Augustine later-than-usual this morning, we were on Saragossa Street near the Saragossa Inn when I asked her, "Do you know what the B&B stands for on their sign."

"Of course. Bed & Breakfast."

"But do you know what an Airbnb is?"

She grinned. "Of course. It's where they pump enriched, highly oxygenated air into your room while you're sleeping to provide a simulated high, sending you into a virtual reality where you're traveling through time and space. You can be there to witness Pedro Menéndez de Avilés landing on the shores of St. Augustine in 1565, or see Henry Flagler open the Hotel Ponce de León in 1888, then wake refreshed and ready to go in the present."

"You don't expect me to believe that, do you?"

"If you do, I'm calling the men to cart you off."

July 23, 2017

While walking Guen through the historic streets of St. Augustine this morning, we were near the corner of Riberia and Carrera streets when Guen said, "What's with all the small, white flags in the ground? Did this yard surrender?"

I nodded. "Yes, Guen, it was an epic battle between St. Augustine grass and Bahiagrass. The St. Augustine grass won."

"Well, of course," she said. "The St. Augustine grass had home field advantage."

July 24, 2017

While walking Guen through the historic streets of St. Augustine this morning, she paused to cool off in a puddle of water. I said, "This reminds me, in the spirit of Michael Phelps racing a great white shark last night to kick off *Shark Week*, I think I'll race something."

"You mean like an earthworm or a dung beetle? Or will you challenge something you have a chance against?"

"Hey, that's not fair. I ran the Gate River Run twice."

She nodded, "Yes, and since then, you partied like it was 1999, because it really was."

"Okay, so it's been 20 years. I bet I can still move."

"No, you have movements."

I sighed, "Maybe you're right. I should probably race to finish this manuscript that we have due to the publisher next week."

"And I'll be on the sidelines cheering for you."

July 27, 2017

While walking Guen through the historic streets of St. Augustine this morning, we were on Cordova Street near Hot Shot Bakery when she pointed to their sign and asked, "What's your favorite type of pastry?"

"That's easy. Pies."

"Um, can you be more specific?"

"Okay, if I had to pick one, I'd say cherry pie. What about you? What's your favorite pastry?"

"Pastries," she responded.

"Um, can you be more specific?"

"Nope."

"Way to narrow it down, Guen."

July 29, 2017

While walking Guen through the historic streets of St. Augustine this morning, we reached the Castillo de San Marcos on the bay.

"When was this fort built?" she asked.

"It was erected by the Spanish between 1672 and 1695."

"Did Antonio Banderas help?"

"Of course not."

"But he's Spanish."

"It was long before his time."

"If he had worked on the construction crew, I would have come here to watch."

"Guen, it was long before your time, too."

She shook her head. "Geez, you're such a pessimist."

July 31, 2017

Before walking Guen through the historic streets of St. Augustine this morning, I overheard Guen whispering to Missy.

"Okay, remember the plan. We need to convince him to take us on extra-long walks today because we missed going yesterday due to the rain. Missy? Missy? Why am I talking to your butt?"

August 2, 2017

While walking Guen through the historic streets of St. Augustine this morning, we were outside Burger Buckets on the corner of Orange Street and Cordova Street when she asked, "What's this game called?"

"Cornhole. You separate the two boards by about a dozen feet, stand near one board, then try and toss bean bags in the hole in the other board."

"What fun is that? Look, I'll tell you how to improve this game. First, replace the bean bag with a tennis ball. Then, one player throws it as far as they can—preferably not into traffic—and the second player retrieves it."

"Guen, that's called fetch."

"Still the best game ever."

August 3, 2017

While walking Guen through the historic streets of St. Augustine this morning, we were on Cordova Street across from Flagler College, formerly the Hotel Ponce de León.

"I would have liked to stay there for a night when it was Flagler's hotel," she said.

"Couldn't. Rooms were rented for the entire season, approximately January through April. No one-night stays."

"I bet that was expensive."

"It was. Only the rich and famous traveling from the north, tycoons of industry, actors, politicians, and the like could afford it. As a matter of fact, it's said that no one living in St. Augustine ever stayed there."

She tilted her head. "Why would someone living in St. Augustine spend time in a hotel in St. Augustine?"

"You know, I've never considered that."

August 6, 2017

While walking Guen through the historic streets of St. Augustine this morning, we were in the circle drive near the Visitor Information Center when Guen found a tall bowl. She suddenly whipped around. With fear in her eyes, she scanned the area in every direction.

"What's the matter?" I asked.

"I don't want to come across the dog who can drink out of this water bowl!"

August 9, 2017

While walking Guen through the muggy, historic streets of St. Augustine this morning, we were on Hypolita Street when she stopped and looked inside a business window for over a minute.

"Yes, Guen, the sign does say Dos Gatos, but no, there are no cats inside."

"I was hoping to see Puss in Boots."

"Guen, Puss in Boots is a cartoon figure."

"Well, he's a cat, and he's Spanish."

"No, the man who does his voice in the *Shrek* movies, Antonio Banderas, is Spanish."

She silently grinned.

Then I understood. "You're hoping Antonio Banderas is in there, aren't you?"

"Si, Señor!"

August 10, 2017

While walking Guen through the historic streets of St. Augustine this morning, we were on San Marco Avenue when she said, "Why do all the moms look so happy as they load their kids into cars this morning?"

"Yesterday was the last day of summer vacation. School starts today, which means moms don't have to put up with immaturity all day long. They might even get in a nap. Moms aren't just happy, they're giddy."

"I totally get it. It's like when you go off for the day."

"Exact—wait, what?"

August 14. 2017

While walking Guen through the historic streets of St. Augustine this morning, we were on the grounds of Fire Station 1 when I said, "Guen, Henry Flagler donated this fountain in 1889."

"If you consider all the structures he built and the things he donated, he did a lot for St. Augustine."

"He was a very benevolent man. As a matter of fact, as he expanded his railroad downstate in the early 1900s, the folks were so grateful that they offered to name a town Flaglerville after him. But Flagler shunned personal attention and turned them down. Instead, the town was named Miami."

"Too bad," she began. "The Flaglerville Dolphins has a nice ring to it. Oh, and for the record, if anyone wants to name an area 'Guenville', I won't stop them."

August 15, 2017

While walking Guen through the historic streets of St. Augustine, we ventured all the way to Plaza de la Constitución before heading back toward the house.

"I'm disheartened," Guen said.

"Why?"

"All the times we've walked King Street, and not once have I ever seen a king."

"That's ridiculous, Guen. That's like saying in all the times we've walked Treasury Street, you've never found a treasure."

Her eyes narrowed. "That was going to be my next gripe."

August 18, 2017

While walking Guen through the historic streets of St Augustine this morning, she turned to me excitedly. "One more day, right?"

"Yep. Flagler College students officially move in tomorrow."

"I'm so excited. It's like Christmas. You know, except for the decorations, holly, lights, presents, Christmas trees—"

"I get it, Guen."

"—eggnog, carols, Santa Claus, reindeer—"

"You've made your point, Guen."

"—chestnuts, *The Nutcracker*, wrapping paper, sleigh rides—"

"You've never been on a sleigh ride."

"I've taken a pedicab. It's the same thing."

"Wait. When did you take a pedicab?"

"You're not always awake."

August 19, 2017

While walking Guen through the historic streets of St Augustine this morning, we were on the bustling grounds of Flagler College when she said, "Finally. I can't believe it's here! College move-in day. It's like my birthday, April Fool's, and Christmas all rolled up into one."

"You are going to be nice, right?"

"Of course. Truth is, I've become more introspective about what today brings. It's really about the young students and the beginning of their journey on a new path. A foray into broader education where minds are massaged and developed into future world leaders and critical thinkers."

"So, you're not going to try to convince them you're a Bolivian Lollygagger?"

"Not at all." She shook her head. "I'm going with something new, like Peruvian Puddle Pooch, Mongolian Mud Monger, or New Zealand Knucklehead."

August 20, 2017

While walking Guen through the historic streets of St. Augustine this morning, we were on Lemon Street when she turned to me, and said, "You did it again?"

"What?"

"You called me Cujo just as that couple passed by. Why do you do that?"

"Just for fun. I like to see people's reaction."

"Just for fun, I think I'll refer to you as Frankenstein."

"Okay. Point taken."

August 22, 2017

While walking Guen through the historic streets of St. Augustine this morning, we were on the south side of the Visitor Information Center when she said, "I'd never trust this wall."

"Why?"

"Look at it. I've heard of being two-faced, but this is ridiculous."

August 23, 2017

While walking Guen through the historic streets of St. Augustine this morning, we were on Almeria Street when she found a toilet.

"Guen, there's a myth that the toilet was created by a man named Thomas Crapper."

She chuckled. "Funny last name. Hey, is that why humans say they're going to take a—"

I cut her off, "The truth is, it was invented by Sir John Harington, a courtier of Elizabeth of England, in 1596. Hence the reason people say they're going to the 'john.'"

"Here's some info for you. I bet you didn't know that the dog collection device was invented by Paul Poohbag."

"I don't think so, Guen."

August 24, 2017

While walking Guen through the historic streets of St. Augustine this morning, we were on Carrera Street when Guen closed her eyes.

"What are you doing?" I asked.

"So many people seemed enthralled with the eclipse last Monday. I'm simulating the effect. It's not helping. I still don't get all the excitement."

"Me, neither. I read where a couple had a baby on Monday and named her Eclipse."

Guen shook her head in disbelief. "Probably came out backward and mooned everyone in the delivery room."

August 25, 2017

While walking Guen through the historic streets of St. Augustine this morning, we were on Sevilla Street by Flagler College when she turned to me and said, "Today is National Secondhand Wardrobe Day."

She looked me up and down, as if scrutinizing my attire. I was wearing khaki cargo shorts and a green tee shirt with the logo of a pub. "What? Are you trying to tell me something?" I asked.

"Not at all. I just see that you've embraced the day with unbridled exuberance."

August 26, 2017

While walking Guen through the historic streets of St. Augustine this morning, we were on West Castillo when she said, "Wow! Look at this super-duper large oak tree! Can you imagine all the dogs who have lifted their leg to this tree? Must be three centuries worth of pee."

"Um, I prefer not to."

She continued, "The pistory must be amazing."

"The what?"

"The pistory. Pee history. I just made it up."

I shook my head. "I suggest you lose it."

August 28, 2017

Before walking Guen through the historic streets of St. Augustine this morning, I found it curious that she had no interest in eating her breakfast. Then, as we were about to go on our walk and I told her it was misting rain, she was still enthusiastic about going. My first thought was, "Who are you, and what have you done with Guen?"

Once under way, she quickly filled up two doggie bags. We were on Oviedo Street when I nodded in understanding. "I get it now. You didn't eat your breakfast because you didn't have any room left. And rain wasn't going to stop you because Mother Nature was calling."

She looked at me with an expression of relief. "Mother Nature wasn't just calling, she was shrieking like a banshee standing in lava with her hair on fire."

August 29. 2017

She finally did it. Guen weaseled her way into the fire station bay at Fire Station 1 on Malaga Street. I had to carry her home in a bucket because she melted into a puddle. You guys made Guen's day.

September 2, 2017

While walking Guen through the historic streets of St. Augustine this morning, we arrived at the courtyard of Flagler College (formerly the 1888 Hotel Ponce de León.) "Guen, most people don't realize the centerpiece of this fountain depicts a sword plunged into the earth. Flagler did it to pay homage to Ponce de León and his discovery of Florida."

"What I want to know is why it's adorned with frogs and turtles? And what's with all the images, statues, and carvings of lions everywhere in this town? What about dogs?"

"Because calling it the Bridge of Dogs doesn't have quite the same appeal."

She nodded. "I guess you're right. Just like it would be a bad idea to rename the song to, 'Who Let the Frogs Out?' "

September 4, 2017

While walking Guen through the historic streets of St. Augustine this morning, we were in a dirt parking lot on Carrera Street when Guen asked, "Why is it so quiet this morning?"

"It's Labor Day. Many people have the day off."

"Oh, yeah. The day we celebrate all the women who had to endure labor pains. What a great tribute to motherhood."

"No, that's not exactly what the holiday's about. You see, Labor Day is—"

"Well it sure isn't about all the fathers who stood by and said, 'Breathe, dear, just breathe' and then got woozy at the first hint of blood," she cackled.

September 5, 2017

While walking Guen through the historic streets of St. Augustine this morning, we were in the circle drive next to the Huguenot Cemetery fence.

"I wonder," Guen mused.

"What?"

"Is this iron fence meant to keep people out, or zombies in?"

"Don't be ridiculous. There's no such thing as zombies."

"Says you," she said, peering through the fence, "but I still have grave concerns."

September 6. 2017

FYI. There's a chance I won't post a "Guen walking" adventure for the next few days. You can blame that teeny tiny storm called Hurricane Irma headed our way. Please, everyone in the affected areas, stay safe, and if you're told to evacuate, please heed the warning. We'll make sure to bug out if the need arises to ensure the furry creatures in the house are all safe.

Until we meet again…

September 12, 2017

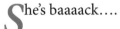 he's baaaack….

    While serpentining our way through the historic, detritus-covered streets of soggy St. Augustine this morning, we were on Cordova Street when Guen said, "That's the problem with hurricanes. For a while, they turn everything upside down."

September, 13 2017

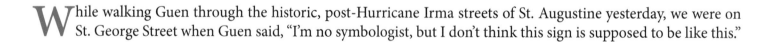

While walking Guen through the historic, post-Hurricane Irma streets of St. Augustine yesterday, we were on St. George Street when Guen said, "I'm no symbologist, but I don't think this sign is supposed to be like this."

September 17, 2017

While walking Guen through the historic streets of St. Augustine this morning, we were on Saragossa Street when I noticed the temperature felt cooler.

"Guen, I believe fall is in the air."

She gave me a sidelong look. "Fall is in the air? How else would something fall if it's not in the air? Sometimes you say the oddest things."

"Um, I meant the season, fall. It's in the air."

"Well of course the season's in the air. Seasons are all about the air temperature. Seriously. Do you hear yourself sometimes?"

"Never mind, Guen."

September 21, 2017

While walking Guen through the historic streets of St. Augustine this morning, we were on King Street when Guen wandered into the entrance of the Casa Monica Hotel parking garage.

"I wonder if I could valet park my car here?" she mused.

"I doubt it," I began, "it's probably only for guests of the hotel."

"Yeah, you're probably right."

"Wait. You don't even have a car, Guen."

"I was waiting to see how long it would take you to come around to that."

September 25, 2017

While walking Guen through the historic streets of St. Augustine this morning, we were outside Francis Field near Riberia Street when Guen asked, "Was the Castillo de San Marcos damaged in the hurricane?"

"Not that I can tell. The fort has survived many hurricanes. Also, in its 322-year history, it's never been taken by force."

"Isn't that the same thing? Hurricane force winds?"

"No, I meant by enemy force."

"I consider Hurricane Irma an enemy. I don't get your point."

I shook my head. "I don't think we're on the same page, Guen."

"I don't think we're in the same library," she scoffed.

September 26, 2017

While walking Guen through the historic streets of St. Augustine this morning, we were at Francis Field when Guen decided to take a break.

Guen spoke, "With Halloween coming in about a month, I'm laser-focused on coming up with a frightening costume."

"How about an IRS auditor?"

"Nah."

"What about dressing up as a zombie dog. You know, a "Walking Dead" walking dog?"

"I need something better."

"How about being a pirate proctologist where your main hand is a hook?"

"Better, but still not great."

"What about dressing up as a cat?"

She looked at me in wide-eyed horror. "You literally just made my skin crawl."

September 30, 2017

While walking Guen through the historic, cloud-shadowed streets of St. Augustine this morning, we were on Cuna Street where she was drinking from a water bowl outside The Social Lounge.

She paused, then asked, "How come it's so windy and overcast?"

"This is the front end of a Nor'easter."

"Is that the same as a hurricane?"

"It's a hurricane's annoying, stinky little brother."

"Please tell me you're not going to make Missy and I go in the back yard tomorrow morning to use the bathroom in a foot of water, like when Hurricane Irma came through."

"That was pretty funny. The entire yard was covered in water. You two walked around for 20 minutes looking for a dry patch of land."

She eyed me with disdain and spoke blandly, "Oh, yeah. Hysterical. A real rib-tickler. On a completely unrelated topic, how are you set with a back-up pair of tennis shoes?"

October 2, 2017

While walking Guen through the historic, puddle-ridden streets of St. Augustine this morning, we were on Cordova Street when she asked, "So you guys have a new book coming out?"

"Yep, after the first of the year."

"Am I in this one?"

"Um, no. They're all fiction."

"Eight novels, and you couldn't find a place for me in any of them?"

"Well, you might say we named an earlier book after you: *Manipulation*."

She glared at me. "I long for the days."

"Huh?"

"When you used to be funny."

October 4, 2017

While walking Guen through the historic streets of St. Augustine this morning, we were at Plaza de la Constitución on King Street when Guen stopped at a fire hydrant.

"Come on, Guen. Let's keep walking."

She didn't move.

"You're a female dog. You don't use a fire hydrant. Why are you stopped?"

"Because."

"We need to get going."

She still didn't move.

"Guen, I know what you're doing. It doesn't mean firemen will be here anytime soon."

"They check hydrants periodically."

"Yeah, but it could be weeks, even months."

"I can wait."

October 6, 2017

While walking Guen through the thoroughly-drenched, historic streets of St. Augustine this morning, we were at Francis Field near the tennis courts when she said, "Wow, it must have rained a lot last night."

"Yeah, and all this water is causing the inlets and river to bulge."

"I wonder," she mused.

"What?"

"If the ocean has ever asked, 'Does this storm surge make my bay look big?' "

October 7, 2017

While walking Guen through the historic streets of muggy St. Augustine this morning, we were at First United Methodist Church on King Street.

"I've never seen white pumpkins," I said.

"They're rare," she began. "They can only be found on Corvo Island in the Portuguese Azores during the last week of September. They're the only type of pumpkin that can be scared to death. That's why they're white."

"You're telling me these are ghost pumpkins?"

"The term 'ghost' is so antiquated. The politically correct phrase is 'substance-challenged,' and don't try to touch the space they occupy. The air is poisonous."

"You expect me to believe all this?"

"Absolutely."

"Even though you just made it up?"

"Absolutely."

October 8, 2017

While walking Guen through the historic streets of St. Augustine this morning, we were traversing the grounds of the Castillo de San Marcos when Guen paused and spoke reflectively, "When the merits and positive attributes of a town can't be summed up in a few sentences, a paragraph, or even a page, you know it's a good place to live."

I was impressed. "That was very aptly put, Guen. You know, you might have a future in writing."

"Nah," she began, "too much work."

October 9, 2017

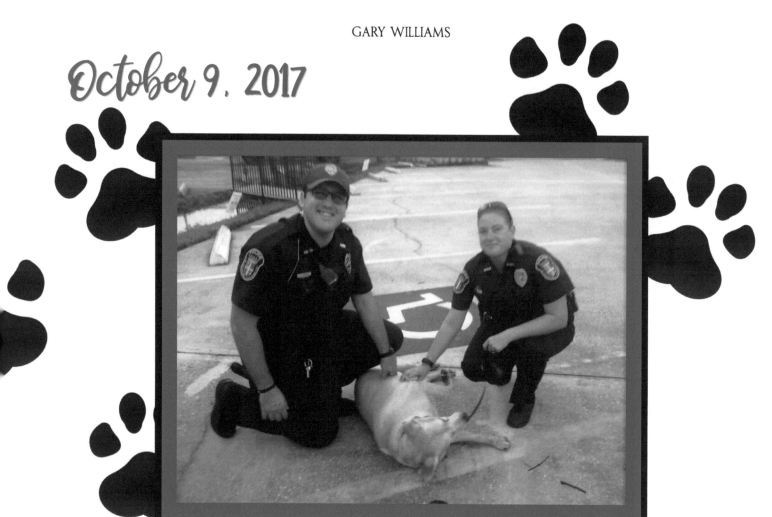

While walking Guen through the historic streets of St. Augustine this morning, we were at First United Methodist Church on King Street when I warned her she was going to get arrested for tromping through the retention ponds. Sure enough, Officer Trotzke and Officer Correa with the St. Augustine Police Department arrived. Guen thought she was about to become a canine convict because she immediately plopped to the ground and assumed the position. Actually, Officer Trotzke (right) recognized Guen from our daily post, and they were gracious enough to stop by and show her some affection. As you can see, she absolutely loved it. Guen now has new friends in uniform.

October 12, 2017

While walking Guen through the historic streets of St. Augustine this morning, we were on Spanish Street when she stopped, and said, "In the spirit of the upcoming holiday, I have a creepy riddle for you."

"Shoot."

"What has six legs, sets out for walks while it's still dark, isn't originally from St. Augustine, but moved here four years ago?"

"Gee, Guen, that's a hard one. The answer is…us."

"Nope. It's the St. Augustine Nocturnal Transcendent Alien."

"Wait, that acronym spells SANTA."

"I said upcoming holiday. I didn't say which one. And on a completely unrelated topic, I heard the pet store is having an early Christmas sale on dog toys this weekend."

65

October 13, 2017

While walking Guen through the historic streets of St. Augustine this morning, we were chatting on Sevilla Street when she stopped dead in her tracks, and said, "Wait. You're telling me that someone is nominating you in St. Augustine Social Magazine for 'St. Augustine's Person of the Year' award?"

"Yeah, for my posts on Facebook. I'm honored just to be considered."

"But I'm the funny one."

"You may find this hard to digest, Guen, but there are a few people who don't believe you talk."

"Helloooo? What am I doing right now?!"

October 16, 2017

While walking Guen through the historic streets of St. Augustine this morning, we were on St. George Street when Guen exclaimed, "Wow! This place sells swords!"

"What would you want with a sword?"

"Well, I'd sink it up to the hilt in a stone. Then, if anyone could pull it out, they'd become King of St. Augustine. You know, like in that MacArthur story."

"Uh, huh. Three things. First, St. Augustine doesn't have a king. Second, MacArthur landed in the Philippines during World War II. You mean Arthur, like in the Arthurian Legend. And third, how are you going to get the sword in the stone?"

There was an awkward moment of silence. "I haven't thought that part through yet."

October 17, 2017

While walking Guen through the windy, soggy, dark, historic streets of St. Augustine this morning, we were cutting through the public parking garage on Cordova Street when she asked, "How old is this structure?"

"Eleven, maybe twelve years old."

"That can't be."

"Why?"

"It looks like an old building. There's no air conditioning, no heating, no indoor plumbing, the walls are cement and appear unfinished."

"It's only for automobiles, Guen. People don't live in here."

"Automobiles need comfortable places, too. I have to say, I never thought you'd be one to car-bash."

"And…this conversation is over."

October 18, 2017

While walking Guen through the historic streets of St. Augustine this morning, we were at Fire Station 1 on Malaga Street. Guen had been giggling for the last three streets. "Let me make sure I remember this correctly," she began. "You told that Flagler freshman that my breed is a Puerto Rican Pilsner Pup."

"Si," I said dejectedly.

"And then she responded, and I quote, 'No she's not. That's a yellow Labrador retriever. It's a retriever in the class of sporting dogs. They're one of the most popular breeds in the U.K. and the U.S. The first yellow Labrador was born in 1899. The breed was formally recognized by the Kennel Club of the U.K. in 1903."

I nodded. "I guess the high school kids going into college are smarter these days."

"Little bit."

October 19, 2017

While walking Guen through the historic streets of St. Augustine this morning, we were on St. George Street. I was carrying two doggie bags. One was filled with a present Guen gave me shortly after leaving the house. The other contained a bottle of water and a bowl for Guen when she gets thirsty. We approached a woman who seemed mortified that I was carrying two full bags.

I pointed to Guen and spoke, "She judged a spicy chili-eating contest last night. She may have sampled a tad too much."

The woman looked at me aghast and wordlessly strolled passed us. I'm not positive, but I think I heard Guen snicker.

October 20, 2017

While walking Guen through the historic streets of St. Augustine this morning, we were between the public parking garage and the Visitor Information Center when I said, "This is the area where the San Marco Hotel once stood. Henry Flagler and his wife, Ida Alice, honeymooned here in 1885. The hotel was lost to a fire in 1897."

"Speaking of the Visitor Information Center, they need to build a PEA."

"Which, if we keep walking, is something I'm going to need to take."

"No, a Pet Expert Area. With a staff to answer tourist questions about local dog parks, emergency veterinary clinics, shops that cater to pets—like the stores with a WIDE variety of animal treats."

"Actually, Guen, that's not your worst idea. Would you settle for it being a subsection of the current Visitor Information Center?"

"Everything's negotiable."

October 22, 2017

While walking Guen through the historic streets of St. Augustine this morning, we were at the basketball courts outside of Francis Field when I instructed her to take a right at the pole.
She thought she was funny.

October 24, 2017

While walking Guen through the historic streets of St. Augustine this morning, we were in the public parking garage when she turned back to look at the toll booths. "I'd like to work here one day. It'd be cool to meet all the people parking here."

"And just think, Guen, if you did, you might not have to go on walks to find people with treats. They might bring them right to you in the toll booth."

Her eyes glazed over. "Be still my beating heart. This has to be the bestest job in the world."

October 25. 2017

While walking Guen through the historic streets of St. Augustine early this morning, we were looking at the pumpkins outside First United Methodist Church on King Street.

"Guen, it's ironic that when this current church was built in 1911, it was painted orange, so people referred to it as the 'pumpkin' church. And now it sells pumpkins at Halloween."

"No, what would be ironic is, now that the building is painted yellow, if people started carving bananas for Halloween."

October 28, 2017

While walking Guen through the historic streets of St. Augustine this morning, we were on Francis Field when I said, "Remember yesterday when I told you about the pieces of Henry Flagler's mansion that the citizens of St Augustine co-opted into their own homes?"

"Vaguely."

"At the south end of St. George Street, there's a house with several fanlight windows from Kirkside. As a matter of fact, it was the home of professional baseball player, Bill Steinecke."

"Wow, a former pro. Did he have a lot of home runs?"

"Well, no. As a matter of fact, during his entire career he only got up to bat four times in 1931."

She cocked her head. "He made four plate appearances and he's still considered a professional baseball player? By that measure, given the times I've led you through the streets before you were completely awake, I should be considered a service animal."

November 1, 2017

While walking Guen through the historic streets of St. Augustine this morning, we were outside Huguenot Cemetery when Guen said, "It's not fair that they only have Halloween for human kids."

"Let it go, Guen."

"They should have a Halloween just for pets. You know, where we can go around from house to house and get treats. I'd dress up as Edgar—the superhero Dachshund—with a black cape and gray fedora, who flies around town helping other pets in need with my magic wand tail."

"Guen, every morning when we walk, people give you treats. I'd say you celebrate Halloween 365 days a year."

She was momentarily silent. "You may have a point. But I'd still like to dress up as Edgar."

November 2, 2017

While walking Guen through the dark, historic streets of St. Augustine this morning, we were on Francis Field. She began sniffing the ground intently. No doubt, she had discovered a morsel of food. Thus, I did what I always do. I nudged her away and placed my foot on top of it so she couldn't eat it. But because of the darkness, I did so blindly. At first, I felt it. Then, I smelled it. That's when I realized my mistake.

She turned to me. "That wasn't food. It's a gift from another dog."

Even in the faint light I could see her laughing.

Daylight Savings Time can't get here fast enough.

November 3, 2017

While walking Guen through the historic streets of St. Augustine this morning, we were on Carrera Street when Guen found a basketball.

She turned to me. "Looks like Lebron James lost his game."

"You know, Guen, Lebron's nickname is King James. And for reasons I still can't comprehend, some people refer to you as Queen Guenevere."

She looked surprised. "What people?"

"Some people."

"Which ones?"

"People."

"I'd like to meet these people."

November 4, 2017

While walking Guen through the historic streets of St. Augustine this morning, we were outside Francis Field when I said, "Guen, Nights of Lights kicks off two weeks from tonight. It marks the official start of the St. Augustine holiday season."

"Oh, that reminds me. I made my Christmas list last night. It's only 19 pages."

"Nineteen pages?!"

"Don't worry. There's only a dozen items on each page."

"Guen, you realize things like renaming Francis Field after you, an unlimited supply of bacon, and your own personal fireman are not viable gifts, right?"

"No problem."

"Really?"

"Yeah, because I have no idea what the word 'viable' means."

November 5, 2017

While walking Guen through the historic streets of St. Augustine this morning, we were on Riberia Street when Guen asked, "You know what today is?"

"Sunday."

"It's also 'National Get Everything on Your Dog's Christmas Shopping List Day.'"

"You just made that up, Guen."

"No, I didn't. It's on page 4 of my shopping list. I requested that you make November 5th 'National Get Everything on Your Dog's Christmas Shopping List Day.'"

"Even if it's on your list, that's an impossible request. And if I could get it, it's November 5th. I haven't gotten your presents yet."

"You're telling me," she grumbled.

"Guen, are you sticking your tongue out at me?"

November 8, 2017

While walking Guen through the historic streets of St. Augustine last Saturday morning, we were traveling up West Castillo Drive when Guen started singing, "Follow the yellow brick road." She paused and said, "Doesn't have quite the same appeal, does it?"

"Well, it's not yellow, it's white. It's not brick, it's concrete. It's not a road, it's a sidewalk. Oh, and you're about the size of 14 Totos."

She glared at me, then started off at a trot.

"What's your rush, Guen?"

"We still have to find you a brain."

November 9, 2017

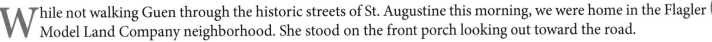

While not walking Guen through the historic streets of St. Augustine this morning, we were home in the Flagler Model Land Company neighborhood. She stood on the front porch looking out toward the road.

"Guen, we're not going walking again this morning."

She turned to me. "I understand."

"I appreciate that, Guen. One more day, and I should feel well enough…wait…are you sticking your tongue out at me again?"

November 10, 2017

Before walking Guen through the cool, historic streets of St. Augustine this morning, she said, "You've had a cold for four days. Aren't you getting better?"

"Very slowly. It's like this virus has separation anxiety and doesn't want to let go."

"I'd say it's more like a stalker. Maybe you could get a restraining order from the courts before you wind up on one of those television shows. On a positive note, at least you got your flu shot last month so you won't get sick."

"In case you weren't aware of it, Guen, your words are dripping with irony."

"Oh, I'm aware."

November 12, 2017

While walking Guen through the historic streets of St. Augustine this morning, we were on Spanish Street. Guen said, "Seeing that bed & breakfast ahead gives me an idea. For Halloween, instead of a bed & breakfast, they should rename it a Dead & Breakfast, and the proprietors can dress up as zombies."

"Let me guess, each guest gets a complimentary corpse?"

"Exactly."

"Not a bad idea, Guen, but we're past Halloween. It was almost two weeks ago."

"Oh, I didn't realize. It's been that long since we've taken a walk."

"It has not!"

November 14, 2017

While walking Guen through the historic streets of St. Augustine this morning, we were on Sevilla Street when she decided to take a rest.

"Guen, have I ever told you how much I love Thanksgiving? As a matter of fact, now that I'm older, I love it more than Christmas."

"That's your problem."

"My mouth waters just thinking about that juicy turkey, mashed potatoes, gravy, and stuffing."

"Eaaaasy, big boy."

"The green bean casserole, cranberry sauce, buttermilk biscuits, and topping it all off with a big slice of pumpkin pie slathered with Cool Whip."

"Careful, I think you're having an out-of-body experience."

"C'mon, let's go," I said, moving off with an extra pep in my step.

Guen ran to catch up. "You better be careful or you're going to pull a giblet."

November 15, 2017

While walking Guen through the historic streets of St. Augustine this morning, we were on the grounds of Flagler College when she said, "With Thanksgiving coming, I hear people talking about all sorts of casseroles: squash casserole, spinach casserole, green bean casserole, broccoli casserole. What's with all the casseroles? And, really, what is a casserole?"

"I don't know, Guen."

"No one does. The casserole is the great enigma. Where did casseroles come from? Who invented casseroles? Will casseroles take over the planet one day?"

I was momentarily quiet. "You just like saying the word 'casserole' don't you?"

"It makes my tongue tingle."

November 16, 2017

While walking Guen through the historic streets of St. Augustine this morning, we were at the Ancient City Baptist Church dirt parking lot on Carrera Street when I found a blue bag. I picked it up, placed my hand inside, and used it like a puppet.

"Look, Guen. Do you see the giant Cookie Monster? It's come to eat your face."

"Actually, I see a man who's going to need therapy when he discovers that dog bag was previously used, then emptied," she said, pointing to the lumps on the ground nearby.

November 17, 2017

While walking Guen through the historic streets of St. Augustine this morning, we were at the south end of Spanish Street when she said, "Huh, I wonder why that lady walked away in a huff?"

"The better question is, why did you greet her with, 'Good morning. I suggest you go take a hike.' "

"Hey, you're the one who told me today is National Take a Hike Day."

I thought about it for a moment. "Yeah, I guess that one's on me."

November 20, 2017

While walking Guen through the chilly, historic streets of St. Augustine this morning, we were on Francis Field when Guen said, "I LOVE this weather."

"Brrr," I responded.

"What do you mean? This is wonderful."

"Brrr."

"It's so invigorating."

"Brrr."

"You know, for a writer, your vocabulary is extremely limited. You might want to buy a vowel."

"It's cold, Guen."

"I knew you could do it. Talkin' in whole words again. I'm proud of you."

"Brrr."

She rolled her eyes. "And then…he regressed."

November 23, 2017

While walking Guen through the historic streets of St. Augustine…actually, when I asked Guen this morning, "Do you want to go for a walk?"

She responded with, "You can't be serious. It's raining Persians and Poodles."

"Huh?"

"Cats and dogs."

So instead, we ventured into the back yard where she took refuge on the couch in the cabana. Almost immediately, she struck her seasonal I-can-smell-turkey-cooking pose. So although there'll be no long walk this morning (no finding furniture by the side of the road, no finding women's clothes, no brides to photobomb, etc.), Guen and I are thankful for every walk we've taken and the adventures awaiting us on future walks. We're especially thankful for all our family and friends, including all the wonderful people we've come to know on Facebook. We hope everyone has a fantastic Thanksgiving, even if it *is* raining Siameses and Shepherds.

November 24, 2017

While swimming Guen through the historically soggy streets of St. Augustine this morning… Just kidding. She wouldn't budge. Too much rain. But we did get in a brief walk yesterday afternoon between the showers, and Guen discovered a stack of timber at Memorial Presbyterian Church on Sevilla Street.

"Looks like they took care of a downed tree," I commented.

"Yeah, right," she said suspiciously. "You know as well as I do they're secretly building an ark. You need to get online and book us reservations before the rain picks up again."

"Sure thing, Guen. Should I upgrade us to the Noah Balcony Suite?"

"Don't be ridiculous. We'd get wet on a balcony."

"Gee, what was I thinking?"

She shook her head back and forth. "I'm never sure."

November 26, 2017

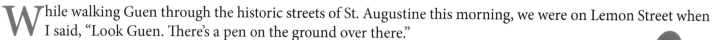

While walking Guen through the historic streets of St. Augustine this morning, we were on Lemon Street when I said, "Look Guen. There's a pen on the ground over there."

"Where?"

"Over there. It's a pen, Guen. Get it? A penguen."

"But penguin is spelled with an 'i' not an 'e' so this makes no sense."

"It's just a joke, Guen."

"Tell that to the penguins whose name you just butchered."

November 27, 2017

While walking Guen through the foggy, historic streets of St. Augustine this morning, we were in the courtyard at the north end of St. George Street where she found a red sleigh and a decorated tree.

"You know what four weeks from today is?" she asked.

"Your birthday?"

"Nope."

"My birthday?"

"I have no idea. But that's not what I'm thinking of. I'll give you a hint. Think red and white guy who's horizontally challenged."

"The Kool-Aid Man."

"No. This guy is pulled around in a sled by eight four-legged animals."

"Oh, you mean the Iditarod race."

"You're killin' me. Last chance. What does 'holiday cheer' mean to you?"

I nodded. "Now I got it. You're talking about a college football bowl game."

"Grrrrr."

"I'm sorry, Guen, I'm doing my best."

November 30, 2017

While walking Guen through the historic streets of St. Augustine this morning, we were on Riberia Street when I said, "Guen, see that late-1800s, white, two-story house on the opposite corner? John W.L. Crawford once lived there with his wife. His wife was the daughter of Thomas Nash, a political cartoonist who was famous for giving us the images of Santa Claus and Uncle Sam."

"Speaking of Santa Claus, do you really think he has a Naughty & Nice list?"

"Sure."

"I bet you were on the naughty list a few times as a child. I'd put the over/under at five Christmases."

"Guen, why would you say that?"

"You didn't know last Monday was four weeks until Christmas."

"Oh, that," I chuckled, "I was just teasing you."

"That's why I'm reconsidering and putting the over/under at seven…and betting the over."

December 1, 2017

While walking Guen through the historic streets of St. Augustine this morning, we reached Flagler's Memorial Presbyterian Church on Sevilla Street.

"Wow, Guen, remember this pile of cedar we saw a few days ago? It's certainly dwindled down."

She glanced around with concern etched across her face.

"What's the matter?" I asked.

"I'm on the lookout for the three-foot, vicious termites that must be lurking somewhere nearby."

December 3, 2017

While walking Guen through the historic streets of St. Augustine this morning, we were near the Visitor Information Center where Guen conducted her monthly check to ensure the Death Star was still grounded.

"Now that I've been on the cover of a magazine, I'm considering a career as a stand-up comedian. Do you want to hear some of my jokes?" Guen asked.

"No."

"What do you call Lassie on the Florida/Georgia line?"

"No idea."

"A Border Collie. What do you call a male cow at the bottom of a hole?"

I had no response.

"A Pit Bull. What do you call a dog from Dublin who's tired?"

I still had no response.

"Not even a guess? It's an Irish Setter. What do you call a Bald Eagle?"

"Um, a Bald Eagle?"

"No, it's a Beagle. Get it?"

"Guen, let's just stick to the walks."

December 4, 2017

While walking Guen through the historic streets of St. Augustine this morning, we were on Charlotte Street when Guen asked, "Catch 27? What is this place?"

"A great restaurant. Unlike the term catch-22, which is a paradoxical situation that you can't escape because of contradictory rules."

"Sounds like catch-22 is named after our cat, 22."

"Guen, that's not nice. Twenty-two loves you."

"Really? Remember last week when he referred to me as a Yellow Lab Coat Retriever?"

"Yeah, that was kinda funny," I snickered.

December 5, 2017

While walking Guen through the foggy, historic streets of St. Augustine this morning, we were at the east end of Carrera Street when I noticed Guen looked tentative. "What's the matter?"

"It's spooky out here."

"Just think, Guen. We may encounter the ghosts of Christmas past, Christmas present, and Christmas future."

"I'll take the one with the presents. You can have the past and future."

December 6, 2017

While walking Guen through the historic streets of St. Augustine this morning, we were on Hypolita Street admiring the Christmas tree in the window of the Columbia Restaurant. "This reminds me," Guen began, "I know what I'm getting you for Christmas."

"Oh, yeah?"

"Seven pairs of tennis shoes. I figure you can't go two months without saying something that annoys me, so this should get you through the entire year."

"Gee, how thoughtful of you, Guen," I said sarcastically.

She nodded. "What can I say, I'm a giver. I get all wrapped up in the season. Get it?"

December 7, 2017

While walking Guen through the wintry, historic streets of St. Augustine this morning, we were on Valencia Street. Guen had a frightened expression as she watched the Flagler College students pass by.

"Look," she began, "they're all walking slow, like they're in a trance, and no one is making eye contact. Is this the Zombie Apocalypse?"

"Nope. It's the last day of finals."

Guen nodded in understanding. "Ah. They're experiencing the Three C's: concentration, consternation, and constipation."

December 8, 2017

While walking Guen through the historic, chilly tundra of St. Augustine this morning, we were on Cordova Street when I said, "Guen, today is National Ding-A-Ling Day. The idea is that you call someone you haven't heard from in a long time."

"That's nice," she said matter-of-factly as the icy wind brushed her face.

"What? No snappy comeback? No witty response?"

"Can't. I think I froze my sense of humor off."

December 9, 2017

While walking Guen through the subarctic, soggy, historic streets of St. Augustine this morning, we were on Charlotte Street where Guen was admiring a wreath.

Through chattering teeth, I spoke sarcastically, "Let's go for a walk, she said. It'll be fun, she said."

"You're just jealous you don't have a fur coat."

"You know, Guen, nowadays, people frown on others who own real fur."

"Hey, I didn't buy it. It's a single-owner coat."

December 10, 2017

While walking Guen through the historic streets of St. Augustine this morning, we were at the Ancient City Baptist Church dirt parking lot on Carrera Street when Guen sniffed out yet another 1800s hand-forged nail, most likely from the carriage house at the back of Henry Flagler's mansion which used to stand there.

"You really are Indiana Guen," I said.

"Yep, I know old when I see it," she said, staring at me.

For a moment, neither one of us said a word.

"You're not funny, Guen."

Her face broke, and she laughed and laughed.

December 11, 2017

While walking Guen through the historic, it-should-never-be-this-cold-in-Florida-ever streets of St. Augustine this morning, we were on Spanish Street when I said, "Guen, it feels like 31 degrees right now. Although I've heard that the trick to enduring cold is just a case of mind over matter."

"Geez, I'm sorry you're at such a severe disadvantage," she cackled.

December 13, 2017

While walking Guen through the historic streets of St. Augustine this morning, we were on Hypolita Street when I said, "Guen, today is National Day of the Horse, National Cocoa Day, and National Violin Day."

"Whatever."

"I think it's cool they have these days to commemorate people, animals, places, and things."

"You want to impress me? Have a National Horse-Drinking-Cocoa-While-Playing-The-Violin Day. Then you've got something."

"I see your sense of humor has thawed."

December 14, 2017

While walking Guen through the historic streets of St. Augustine this morning, we were on St. George Street where Guen was window shopping. She turned to me. "Twelve days until Christmas, right?"

"Yep, just like the song, which always confused me. Is the first day of Christmas on the 13th, or is that the 12th day of Christmas and you count down from there?"

Guen rolled her eyes. "Does it really matter? Somebody's 'true love' is giving them things like 'lords-a-leaping' and 'maids-a-milking.' The relationship is already in the tank."

December 16, 2017

While walking Guen through the historic streets of St. Augustine yesterday morning, we were on Charlotte Street just past Wolf's Museum of Mystery when I joked, "Just think, Guen, maybe one day they'll have a whole room in that museum dedicated to you."

Her eyes lit up. "Oh, wow. That would be fantaburrific!"

I nodded. "Or maybe a room dedicated to the words you make up."

December 17, 2017

While walking Guen through the historic streets of St. Augustine this morning, we had just come through the public parking garage when I noticed Guen staring at the front of the Visitor Information Center.

"What are you looking at, Guen?"

"That blue circle. Why is there a picture of a man on his knees leaning backward about to tip over?"

"Um, it's an 'I' for 'Information.'"

"Nope, I'm pretty sure it's a man about to tip over backward."

December 18. 2017

While walking Guen through the historic streets of St. Augustine yesterday, we were at the back of Flagler College.

"Guen, when Henry Flagler built the Ponce de León Hotel, the seven rooms on the other side of this loggia were artists' studios. Guests staying in the hotel could visit the studios and shop for paintings. Artists would also teach guests how to paint for a fee. It wasn't that Flagler was an art connoisseur. He simply admired anyone working hard to make a living with their artistic talents."

She didn't respond.

"Guen, did you hear what I said?"

"I'm still trying to figure out what a 'loggia' is. Talk about making up words."

December 20, 2017

While walking Guen through the historic streets of St. Augustine, we were in the Flagler College student parking lot on Carrera Street behind Lewis House.

"Where are all the cars?" Guen asked.

"The college kids have gone home and won't return until after New Year's."

"But what if I get a new collar for Christmas? I'll have no one to show it off to when we go on our morning walks."

"Guen, we just bought you a new collar."

"You can't expect me to wear this one every day. You don't wear the same underwear every day, do you?"

"A collar is not underwear."

"It will be if Santa brings me the firefighter's uniform I asked for."

"For the last time, you won't be able to sneak into a firetruck unnoticed."

"We'll see."

December 22, 2017

While walking Guen through the historic streets of St. Augustine this morning, we were on Carrera Street approaching town when she said, "Christmas is on Monday, right?"

"Yep. And I spoke to Santa Claus last night. He said you have to be especially good to me these last three days in order to get your presents. That includes no sarcastic comments."

Her mind seemed to drift into deep thought. "Wow, that's tough. I'm going to have to go home and map out the pros and cons for that one. Wait. Can your flip phone even reach the North Pole?"

"Um, I'd say that qualifies as a sarcastic statement, Guen."

"I'd argue it's a valid question."

December 23, 2017

While walking Guen through the beautiful, historic streets of St. Augustine this morning, we were outside Herbie Wiles Insurance on the corner of Ponce de León Blvd and Saragossa Street.

"That's odd," Guen said.

"What is?"

"Seeing Santa inside an insurance company."

"Why? Isn't Santa allowed to buy insurance?"

"Don't be ridiculous. Everyone knows he provides his own coverage."

"You mean…?"

"That's right," Guen nodded. "He's elf insured."

December 24, 2017

After walking Guen through the historic streets of St. Augustine this morning, we were on our back porch when Guen said, "I'm so excited! Tomorrow is Christmas! In honor of the day, I've come up with my own 'Twelve Days of Christmas' song, St. Augustine style."

"On the twelfth day of Christmas, my true love gave to me…

Twelve froggie statues (at Flagler College fountain),

Eleven articles of clothing (we've found on the street),

Ten homemade dog treats (from Hot Shots Bakery),

Nine firemen just standing there,

Eight doggie sweaters (from Faux Paws),

Seven days a week (Ann O'Malley's is open),

Six taps of craft beer (at The Social Lounge),

Five tasty stops (on a pub crawl),

Four lions guarding (the Bridge of Lions),

Three statues of pineapples (that we've seen),

Two mannequins with animal heads (freakin' me out on St. George Street),

And a fantaburrific Christmas tree (in the lobby of Flagler College)."

"Not bad, Guen. Not bad at all."

"So, is it time to go to sleep yet?"

"It's 9 a.m., Guen. Probably should wait a few more hours."

December 25, 2017

Before opening presents this morning, Guen and I ventured through the historic streets of St. Augustine. After walking through the Arcade of Professional Artisans and Craftsmen just off St. George Street, we arrived at the grounds of Flagler College.

Guen said, "I think I'd like to be an artist. A painter, maybe."

"You could cut off one ear and be Van Guen."

"I don't have that kind of commitment. Maybe I should rethink this. Besides, it's hard to be an artist. I'd rather do something MUCH easier."

"Like what?"

"Be a novelist."

"You're not funny, Guen. And now you're in trouble. Santa is standing behind you and heard that crack."

"Where!?"

"Gotcha."

December 26, 2017

While walking Guen through the historic, borderline-polar streets of St. Augustine this morning, we were just off Hypolita Street in a small courtyard between Cottonways and Columbia Restaurant. The walkway circled an ornate fountain, and Guen took me around and around it until I finally exclaimed, "Stop! What are you doing?"

"Always thought I'd like to be a lap dog, but I don't see the appeal. This is exhausting, and I'm getting dizzy."

December 27, 2017

While walking Guen through the eerily foggy, historic streets of St. Augustine this morning, we were moving east on Carrera Street when she whipped around and asked, "What was that? Did you see that?"

"Probably just the Ghost of Christmas Two Days Past."

"Not funny."

"It might explain why your front left leg is disappearing."

"Gaaah!"

"Just kidding. You were moving when I snapped the picture."

"I knew that," she said in a voice more frazzled than confident.

December 31, 2017

While walking Guen through the icy, historic streets of St. Augustine this morning, we took a break on the porch of Hot Shots Bakery on Cordova Street.

"So, Guen, tomorrow is the first day of 2018. Have you come up with any New Year's resolutions?"

"As a matter of fact, I have. I think we should do more charitable events, do another fundraiser for Ayla's Acres No-Kill Animal Rescue in the spring."

I smiled. "That's very admirable. Any chance you'll throw in a resolution that I don't have to take you for walks on these cold winter mornings?"

"Sure, there's a chance. There's also a chance I'll give up dog treats, firemen, and attention."

About the Author

Gary Williams lives in St. Augustine, Florida, with his wife, Jackie. When he's not walking Guen, his yellow Labrador retriever, he's writing full time. His passions include history, sports, and fishing.

"Walking Guen," the first book in this series, was published in 2018.

To date, he and his co-writer, Vicky Knerly, have published eight novels and one short story with Suspense Publishing:

Death in the Beginning (The God Tools: Book 1)
Three Keys to Murder
Before the Proof – A Samuel Tolen short story
Indisputable Proof (A Samuel Tolen Novel: Book 1)
Manipulation
Evil in the Beginning (The God Tools: Book 2)
End in the Beginning (The God Tools: Book 3)
Collecting Shadows
Blood Legacy (A Samuel Tolen Novel: Book 2)

If you're interested in becoming a "Guenabler," too, check out all her merchandise at https://www.cafepress.com/guenablermerchandise.

CPSIA information can be obtained
at www.ICGtesting.com
Printed in the USA
BVHW060917141220
595616BV00002B/50

* 9 7 8 0 5 7 8 4 5 7 2 4 6 *